IN
Heaven
KITTENS PLAY

The Blue Angel and Her Garden of Pets

Written by **Nick L. Sacco**

Illustrated by Julie Nixon & David Marak

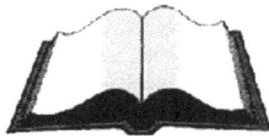

CCB Publishing
British Columbia, Canada

In Heaven Kittens Play:
The Blue Angel and Her Garden of Pets

Copyright ©2010 by Nick L. Sacco
ISBN-13   978-1-926918-15-0
First Edition

Library and Archives Canada Cataloguing in Publication
Sacco, Nick L., 1957-
In heaven kittens play : the blue angel and her garden of pets / written by
Nick L. Sacco ; illustrated by Julie Nixon and David Marak – 1st ed.
Short stories.
ISBN 978-1-926918-15-0
Also available in electronic format.
I. Title.
PS3619.A22I6 2010   813'.6   C2010-906101-2

Original cover art design by Jinger Heaston: www.jingraphix.org

The story *The Blue Angel* contained herein was first published in
Every Cat Has A Story, CCB Publishing, 2007.

Publisher: CCB Publishing
                British Columbia, Canada
                www.ccbpublishing.com

Dedication

I owe a great thanks to my friend Traci for her moral support and guidance in the writing of this book. A special show of appreciation also goes to my animal rescue friends who have offered thoughts, ideas, stories and so many other things to make this book a success. Just as important are all of the wonderful and loving animals that have allowed me the privilege to connect with them.

Testimonials

"The story touched my heart from the beginning and provided a sense of peace to the grief over the loss of a pet."
- Merry Drew

"I found it extremely touching and reassuring that our furry kids are happy and will be waiting for us on the other side."
- Linda Brown

"I was so touched by "In Heaven Kittens Play." I too, have shared my life with many precious pets... most of them rescued. I believe and find comfort that they have a special place to live forever. I thought that Nick did a wonderful job of describing his incredible experiences with the Blue Angel. The only times I found it difficult to read, were the times when I was brought to tears. I found it very engaging and, as a great lover of our innocent animal friends, very comforting about where they go when they leave us. I enjoyed it very much and recommend it highly."
- Debbie Erikson

Contents

Foreword

My first encounter with Nick Sacco occurred while compiling cat stories for a series of books I was writing. He submitted *The Blue Angel and Her Garden of Pets* which truly captivated me with its concept. I was left wondering about an author who could write with such sensitivity and yet had been in active service for his country as a marine.

Nick has a manner of writing that is deeply personal and touching. In his story of the Blue Angel I was drawn to his compassion and left with hope that I too would see the pets I have loved and lost. Likewise, I hope one day to be an angel with my own Garden of Pets. I have always been comforted by "The Rainbow Bridge" but now even more so after reading Nick's work. There is no greater comfort than knowing Tara, Jas, Tia and Tally Ho, to name but a few, are waiting for me when my time comes. I am comforted that my present domestic litter of seven, which I kept when adopting their pregnant mother Karma, will never truly leave me.

Nick has the capacity to leave his readers in tears or amused by the experiences he has shared with his own cats and those he has fortunately rescued. Every story is unique, and every cat is special due to Nick's keen observations of the feline world. You will be deeply moved by Joleen, the mother protecting her 3 kittens in a dirty city dumpster, to Indiana Jones, a one-eyed Abyssinian character who was rescued from an inhumane kitty mill operation. There are also Nick's experiences with the miracle of Thomas O'Mally and Crystal's special gift which was uniquely received from the Blue Angel. Especially touching were Nick's memories of his father and the special dogs he has also loved during his life. Nick's writing is meaningful to me because we share a true spiritual passion for all cats. His love for them virtually seeps through the pages.

In Heaven Kittens Play is written with pure compassion that is touching and leaves the reader wanting more. I was deeply moved while reading this book and reminded of the beloved series of James Herriot's *All Creatures Great and Small*; such is the writing of Nick Sacco. The stories are all true, written by a pet volunteer who with his wife, Alisa, has rescued countless cats, including many abandoned queens and their litters. This is a book you'll read more than once and will also want to share with family and friends. As a cat lover, you will take greater pleasure and see your furry extended family through new eyes once reading these delightful stories. I personally hope this will be the first book of many, for Nick is a gifted writer and this first book left me with a hunger to read more.

Jasmine Kinnear
Feline Behavior Consultant
Author: *Every Cat Has A Story*

Epigraph

*"Heaven's the place where all the cats
you've ever loved come to greet you."*

Chapter One

Lucky the Reptile Hound

My first experience with the death of a pet happened many years ago. I was five or six and lived with my family in St. Louis, Missouri. I recall the experience very vividly, just like you forever carry the memory of a certain event in your life. Some good and some bad but all lay quietly in our minds to be brought back for review when daydreaming or, stimulated by something we see, hear or even smell. Such was the death of my dog Lucky.

Lucky was my dog, a tan, short hair German Shepherd mix with a curly tail that was wagging most of her waking hours and a solid black muzzle. My father had rescued her from the city pound as a young pup, he especially was attracted to her dark face. Dad, a first generation Italian American firmly believed that the darker a dog's muzzle the better the watch dog. He also selected her because when he started down the cage lined hallway Lucky was the first dog to start barking at him.

She jumped around the front of her cage announcing her presence and she was doing exactly what watch dogs should do....watch!

After completing the paperwork Lucky happily rode home in the backseat of Dad's 1960 Ford Falcon. Her muzzle hanging out the partially open window, gums flapping in the wind Lucky maintained a barking assault on any other car, truck or pedestrian that came within range. Once home Mom, in her customary dress and apron, a poor June Cleaver substitute, came out to meet us. For whatever reason, Lucky immediately took a dislike to her. The barking at Mom extended beyond getting attention or guarding her territory. Her tail quit wagging and the hair on her back stood up like the teeth on a comb. Her barking became more deep and menacing, interrupted every few seconds by a growl as if she had just seen the devil himself. Maybe it was the apron or even the bouffant hair, but Lucky didn't like Mom and never would. Though her aggressive posture towards Mom eased over time she never warmed-up to her. I often heard her complaining to Dad that "your damn dog" hid under the bed and growled at her every time she came into the room.

In the wintertime Lucky stayed in the house with us only venturing out into our fenced backyard to do her dog business, chase the squirrels away and bark at any human she could spot as she stood guard upon the top of her dog house. Dad, a carpenter, had built Lucky the *king* of dog houses one weekend. It was roomy by dog standards, made out of solid wood, raised up off the ground, lined with carpet and covered with shingles that Dad had kept from one of his home repair projects. As I would walk up the street from the bus stop after school, there would be Lucky standing proudly on her dog house as if she were Queen-of-the-World. Lucky was always smiling, her entire body shaking in rhythm with her wagging, curly tail and barking her greetings to acknowledge that I had been safely returned by the large yellow dragon that swept me away every morning.

Yes Lucky was a good dog, a playmate, and loved all the kids who came to romp in our yard. She adored my dad, avoided my mother and apparently had a dislike for turtles.

One summer going to my grandparent's farm, we had stopped and collected every box turtle we found crossing the old dusty dirt road that lead to their home, eleven in all. Dad released our box of armored reptiles into our fenced backyard certain they would not be able to escape their wire enclosure. Lucky wasn't quite sure what to make of them. She began by barking at them, then sticking her nose close to their shells to sniff and huff at them. Once or twice she used her paw to flip them around. However, she soon lost interest in them and went on about her business of patrolling the street and barking at the milk delivery man. Apparently, unknown to the humans who lived on Joel Avenue, the milkman, mailman, and anyone else in uniform were out to rob, kill or harm us in some unspeakable manner. We humans were not privy to this covert conspiracy and went about our daily activities in blissful ignorance. Lucky and the other dogs on the block nevertheless maintained their 24-hour vigil.

For the next several days after the turtles were released, all seemed normal. However, we began to notice that our turtle herd was shrinking. Dad checked the fence line looking for an opening they had created but discovered nothing. Eleven turtles became nine. Nine became six. The mystery of the missing turtles would continue for another week until one morning Mom, doing dishes and looking out the window spotted Lucky carrying an object in her mouth prancing happily through the grass. Peering closer Mom realized that Lucky held in her mouth the last surviving box turtle of the group. Nearing a large oak in the yard which supported an old rope and wood swing, she gently placed the

turtle down and began to dig a hole. She continued her efforts, paws and dirt flying until she was satisfied her excavation was complete. Then tail held high she picked the turtle up, dropped it squarely in the freshly dug hole and then to the shock of my watching mother began to bury it. Screaming and yelling Mom immediately raced out the backdoor in an effort to save the box turtle from being buried alive. Lucky, it turned out, would have nothing to do with these lifesaving measures and stood her ground against the crazed, dishtowel swinging housewife. Mom would eventually retreat to the house and call Dad at his office to report that his "damn dog had buried a turtle."

That afternoon, as I neared the house after school, Dad driving his blue company car overtook me. "Get in," he yelled, leaning across the seat to open the door. As he screeched into our driveway like something from the Dukes of Hazzard, he leapt from the car while ordering me to grab a shovel and meet him in the backyard. I didn't know why but I could sense urgency in his voice. Dad, who didn't speak any English until he was three years old, was yelling in a combination of English and Italian accompanied by lots of hand waving. We children had learned years ago this combination of actions signaled that Dad was excited, arguing with Mom or drunk. Not quite sure what was going on yet, I followed orders, wearing my required parochial school uniform of black pants, white shirt and toting a Bat Man lunchbox. The shovel raised high over my head like a soldier wading a river, I soon found Dad and Mom standing in the backyard staring at a spot in the ground. Lucky on the other hand sat between them, tail wagging with a big goofy grin on her face. Mom kept yelling and pointing at Lucky, Dad kept yelling and waving his arms as if he were on fire. Lucky sat beside a freshly dug piece of earth, smiling up at Dad one moment and then looking up at Mom with a glare and a growl. Snatching the shovel I was holding, Dad began digging, tossing a cloud of dirt behind him as he worked. With blazing speed he exposed a shallow depression in the ground. Kneeling down he began to scoop at the dirt with his hand. Lucky, thinking help was required shoved her nose where Dad was trying to work and began digging, tossing the remaining dirt between his legs hitting the top of Mom's shoes which drew another "damn dog" comment from her. Urging Lucky away, Dad felt around in the hole and removed the dirt-encased turtle. Hopping around on her back legs, Lucky began sniffing at the rescued turtle that Dad now held, closed up tight in its shell. We feared it was dead.

For some reason, Dad began shaking it back and forth like someone would do to an unwrapped present. Whether by accident or not, it worked. By some reptilian means, his head slowly poked out, followed a second later by his feet making a swimming motion in mid air. All in the group went silent. Dad placed the turtle in the grass where he crawled off, as if nothing had happened. At dinner that evening, Dad determined that newly named "George-the-Turtle" needed a change of scenery. Continuing to live in the backyard with Lucky, "The Executioner of Reptiles" would only end badly.

The following weekend George-the-Turtle would be returned to my grandparent's farm. Some years later I overheard my tough old grandmother complaining that something was eating her tomatoes and she suspected a turtle. At the young age of five, I immediately knew that it had to be George-the-Turtle happily stuffing himself without the fear of being entombed alive by an overzealous German Shepherd.

During the better weather of the spring and summer Lucky was very content to remain outside where she often slept atop her dog house. With no more turtles to terrorize most of her daily activity was holding court every morning with the squirrels and birds who lived in the backyard, and barking a greeting to the elderly Austrian lady who lived beside us. Then one morning I noticed that Lucky wasn't at her normal post on the roof of her house. I opened the back door and stepped onto the concrete porch calling her name. Usually she was immediately at your feet, jumping on you, biting your ankles, tugging at your sleeve or kissing your face with big wet swipes of her black tongue. This day was different, and as I gazed around the yard there was no Lucky to be found. My first thought was that she had escaped her yard. She had done it once or twice before which led to a massive search by my parents, sisters and a small volunteer army of neighborhood kids. As I turned to race inside and sound the alarm something behind the dog house stopped me in my tracks. There lay Lucky, silent, unmoving. I began to call out her name trying to raise her from her slumber, to no avail. Slowly, cautiously I eased myself towards her. She lay on her side, her back resting against the wall of her home, eyes closed as if sleeping. Fear and panic of these events which I could not understand enveloped me. My screams for help quickly brought my parents barreling out of the house to my rescue. Picking me up my mother carried me inside as my eyes stayed locked on my father as he kneeled down and gently laid his hand on Lucky's body.

Standing looking through the backdoor, I remember feeling fear and confusion as to what had happened. Why wouldn't Lucky wake up? Why did my parents seem sad? My six-year-old mind needed answers to understand. After a few minutes my dad entered the house. He had been ready for work, white shirt and dark pants, his daily office attire. "Nicky Lee, come with me," he said, putting a hand on my shoulder and guiding me into the living room. Having referred to me with both my first and middle name could only mean something serious. He sat his solid, muscular frame on the floor next to me and, eye-to-eye explained that Lucky had just gotten old and died. He then told me something that would stick with me to this day. Lucky had gone to "Doggy Heaven." As if an expert on the hereafter, Dad explained how doggy heaven was a wonderful place of woods and grass and trees where all dead doggies went to live. There were cats to chase all day and every place they dug would turn up a bone. It was a paradise for deceased dogs and I remember feeling great relief knowing that Lucky now lived in such a perfect place in Heaven. I often wondered what Lucky would do without being able to growl at Mom and having an endless supply of turtles to bury.

Wiping away tears from my young face, little did I know that decades later, "Doggy Heaven" would take on a whole new meaning for me.

"How we behave toward cats here below determines our status in heaven."

- Robert A. Heinlein

Chapter Two

Elizabeth and God's Creations

One of my favorite paintings that I own is of Jesus. It's not very fancy and doesn't portray any significant events in his life on earth like the crucifixion or the baptism. It shows him simply holding a lamb in his arms. His expression is soft, protecting and the lamb is calm and peaceful. For some reason this image gives me a great sense of comfort.

I don't pretend to be an expert on theology or for that matter the Bible in general. I am a Christian, attend church weekly and help where I can. I try, with great effort, to live my life as the Lord would want. I'm often called on to give the blessing at family gatherings and two out of three times I can name the majority of the Ten Commandments without messing up. But don't expect me to quote more than one or two Bible verses and there is only one that I can recite word for word.

As a young child I was raised within the Catholic Church in St. Louis, Missouri. Being the youngest of three children with an Italian Catholic father, attending any church other than Roman Catholic was pretty much unheard of. Though I would later escape to the public school system, my two older twin sisters, Tina and Ginny, would serve nearly a twelve-year sentence. They had to wear a uniform consisting of a plaid skirt, white shirt, bobby socks, black & white "Saddle" shoes and a cute little "Doily" looking thing on their heads. Over the years I visited other churches, attended Bible studies and other groups, where I would learn and hear various teachings and opinions on the creation of the world, salvation and the end of times. However, the one thing that no one ever addressed was animals in relationship to the Bible. All of us have visions of the serpent in the Garden of Eden, the farm animals in the manger scene and Noah's Ark. But not once did I ever hear a Priest, Pastor or Minister stand up in front of a congregation and say, "This morning I'm going to talk about what happens to your pet hamster when he dies."

Many people don't put much thought into what happens to a pet when it dies. To them, these creatures either simply grace our dinner table or fill the role of a family pet. Our interaction with our pets consists of feeding them and letting them out. For some uncaring people the animals they have taken in hardly warrant a second thought.

As a Christian I've researched the Bible to learn what importance pets play in it. However, this book isn't written just for those who believe in a certain faith, church or belief. There are many people, like my sister-in-law Elizabeth, who may not claim allegiance to God as we know him but do trust that there is a higher power or creator responsible for all that exists. Elizabeth shares a funny story that as a young child she was kicked out of Sunday school after an argument with the teacher. It seems that the older woman leading the class told Elizabeth, with unquestioned belief that her dog couldn't go to heaven with her when she died. Elizabeth, with equal determination told the Sunday school teacher that her pets would be going to heaven with her. Apparently the two of them came to a compromise that Elizabeth would never return to Bible class again. Instead she would seek her own system of belief which was more accepting of pets in paradise.

The Bible speaks of animals throughout its writings. From the beginning in Genesis animals are mentioned.

> ➢ Genesis 1:21: And God created the great sea animals and the creeping things all having a living soul. God said, let the earth bring forth souls of life according to its kind, the cattle, the beasts of the field, every bird of the heavens according to its kind.

Now some will say this means that animals play a part in life but they don't have souls like us. They aren't worthy of a heavenly afterlife. Again, this is something addressed by the Bible when it talks about the new earth.

> ➢ Isaiah 11:6: The wolf will live with the lamb, the leopard will lie down with the goat, and the calf and the lion and the yearling together. The cow will feed with the bear, their young will lie down together.

As a pet lover myself, I do not or am unable to accept an afterlife or heaven devoid of animals.

> ➢ Corinthians 2:9 says that heaven is a place of happiness beyond imagination where God will give us the desire of our hearts.

Well like my sister-in-law Elizabeth, the desire of my heart is that my pets join me when I die and in heaven I know they will be there.

Does that mean that every pet I've ever owned is going to be with me in the afterlife? I really don't think so. While, as a child, I enjoyed my goldfish, dime store turtles, a handful of mice, hamsters and gerbils plus some "sea monkeys," I don't think everyone is going to be there waiting for me, especially the sea monkeys. They were very disappointing little creatures I purchased out of a comic book when I was young.

Do I think these before mentioned pets go somewhere special when they die? Absolutely. Every creature created by God is important to him. I think a garden awaits them all, as does an angel committed to love and serve them.

But there are pets in our lives who have a very special meaning. For some people this might be something small and furry but almost all of us have shared time in our life with a dog, cat, horse or other animal who holds a very special place in our hearts. I feel these critters will be as much a part of heaven as will be our human friends.

Some people say that an animal can't go to heaven because they don't have a "human" soul, whatever that is. Well I disagree. Everyone has had a pet that expressed emotions. The look on their face and eyes express love, contentment and delight. They look guilty when they've been caught doing something wrong and they can learn and obey commands.

Unlike humans I feel that the souls an animal possess are different from ours, much more innocent and pure. When was the last time a gang of Persian cats planned and knocked over an armored car or a Great Dane conspired to cheat, harm or kill someone...never. Animals, especially those in the wild, not the domesticated pets we have come to know and love, act purely on instinct. Lions don't hunt and kill a gazelle because they hold a grudge, they do it to survive.

So does that mean animals are not important because they have a soul different from ours? No. God created all animals and loves them. From the insects that hop, fly and buzz including, oh yes, even sea monkeys.

"Kittens are angels with whiskers."

- Author Unknown

Chapter Three

The Blue Angel

As volunteers with a cat rescue group, my wife and I often shared our most celebrated success stories with others. An abandoned litter saved, a kitten finds the perfect "forever home," another nursed back to health from the brink of death.

Unfortunately, along with the many stories of success there are all too many stories of sadness. Sick cats left on a doorstep with little chance of survival, pets who have served much of their lives giving unconditional love only to be abandoned in shelters and on the streets, innocent unwanted creatures abused and neglected in innumerable and unfathomable ways. We watch too many of these broken hearted cats simply pine away and die; sad, alone, confused. One wonders what they have done to deserve this fate.

A particular story comes to mind that is at once sad yet inspiring. We had taken in an abandoned mother and her sick kittens that were no more than four weeks old. Despite our best efforts, within three days two of the three had died, and by the third evening we knew the same fate would inevitably claim the last. Serving my country as a Marine coupled with a career in law enforcement has toughened me in many ways, however, I tend to be a soft hearted person when it comes to these moments and I take the death of every kitten probably even harder than my wife who fought so hard to save them.

Late that night as I watched the remaining kitten lie nearly motionless in its cage, I could just not bear the thought that it would leave this world alone. I wrapped it in something warm and cozy, and carried this precious baby up to bed with me. Keeping it cupped in my arm, I laid down with it. The next hour seemed like an eternity as I prayed silently in the dark, listening to the baby struggle and fight for life, jerking every so often and letting out with a small, sad meow. I knew its life was ebbing away as these little gasps at life became fainter and weaker. In my prayers I repeatedly asked God, "What happens to the kittens when they die?" As a Christian I understand the concept of salvation and heaven, but I found myself wondering about these innocents. What happens to them? Where do they go? What awaits them?

During my vigil of prayers, still holding this nearly lifeless kitten, I drifted off to peaceful slumber surrounded by my thoughts and prayers. I awoke sadly, immediately sensing the kitten was gone, but still feeling a presence of sorts filling the room. As I sat up and allowed my eyes to focus I was surprised to see a woman standing near me at the foot of my bed. What some may call a vision or a dream was as clear and real to me as anything I hold dear, and remains as clear to me today as when I first awoke. I felt no fear, only a sense of peace.

The woman appeared to be middle aged, with delicate features and chestnut hair that was parted in the middle and gathered in a bun. A flowing sash the warm color of blue sage was draped over her shoulders accenting her soft azure gown that billowed as if in a gentle breeze. The air inside the room remained still and silent. I immediately knew in my heart that this must be an angel. Her gentle smile instantly warmed me to the depths of my soul. I paused for a moment to take it all in. It was then that I realized that in her hands she was holding the small kitten who I had just held and comforted in its last moments of life. This small kitten of powder white innocence, however, was not the sickly, suffering, abandoned animal of a short while ago. Its coat was healthy and shined,

blue eyes bright and clear, and it rolled and purred in the woman's hands in ways it never had the luxury of doing before.

The scene suddenly transformed and I found myself no longer within the confines of my own bedroom, but in the most beautiful garden eyes have ever seen. Birds and insects flew every which way; wonderfully fragrant flowers and trees of all sorts grew in every direction, as lush meadows and azure ponds dotted the landscape.

The "Blue Angel" sat patiently watching my wonder and amazement from across a small brook. She began to speak in a voice as soft as a harp's song. She explained that she had been sent to me to answer the questions I had presented in my prayers that night. She told me how every living thing is equally important to God because they were created by his hand. Quoting Matthew 10:29 she said, "Not a single sparrow can fall to the ground that the Father does not know it." She then said to me the thing that most struck my heart: "I am an angel who has chosen to serve here in the Garden of Pets by my own request." In an instant, without further explanation, I understood that every pet that dies goes to their own special garden where a truly special angel awaits them. Together they will remain with the angel, caring for, playing with and forever loving them until the day comes to pass that the pet's one and true human companion comes over to join them. "But what if a pet doesn't have a special human companion?" I asked, and the angel simply replied, "Then we stay together here forever," she said smiling. As the scene began to fade, images surrounding the Blue Angel became apparent, images of many kittens and older cats. Some slept soundly; some played in the lush green meadow chasing butterflies and tackling each other; and as any proper cat must do, some groomed lazily in the sunlight. Many of the kittens I could recognize as ones who had touched my life in some way before they died, and in my last image of the Blue Angel I saw her place the little white kitten on the ground as her two siblings raced up to pounce excitedly upon their sister.

Since that time I've continued to have visits from the Blue Angel during my dreams. Often these visits come after the loss of a cat or kitten for which I held a close, personal affection. It's as if she wants to reassure me that all is well. The Blue Angel's garden was a busy one as I watched happy, healthy, beloved kittens run and play around her. Whenever I've had the privilege of visiting it, I always awake with a feeling of inner peace knowing these babies will be there waiting for the day when my turn comes to meet with the Blue Angel and collect my cherished souls.

Each year there are still sad times that come along with all the good, and sadly there will always be kittens that can't be saved and each loss still hits me as hard as the last, but I am comforted knowing the Blue Angel awaits them. As I write down these thoughts I know a new kitten season is upon us and that many sick babies and lost souls are just beyond the horizon. Many kittens, like the one who first led me to the Blue Angel, will come into my life as theirs nears the end. I've adopted a firm belief that no kitten deserves to ever die alone, never knowing what it is to be loved. So when the end nears I'll wrap them up warm and safe and sit with them in my rocker. I'll hold them close and through the tears will softly whisper comforting stories of the Rainbow Bridge, the Blue Angel who is waiting for them in the meadow that lies before it, and the wonders that lie beyond. Eventually the end will come and they'll be laid to rest in my own personal garden of kittens behind our home, which, though quiet and peaceful is nowhere as beautiful as the garden to which their souls have already passed on.

"A kitten is the most irresistible comedian in the world. Its wide-open eyes gleam with wonder and mirth. It darts madly at nothing at all, and then, as though suddenly checked in the pursuit, prances sideways on its hind legs with ridiculous agility and zeal."

- Agnes Repplier

Chapter Four

Joleen the Nursemaid

After my privileged introduction to the Blue Angel, her visits to me and lessons would continue. On some occasions the loss of a close pet would lead to a visit as I slept. Other times while awake, the angel would appear to simply share a comforting thought or vision with me. Most often, though, my prayers for knowledge about this wonderful Garden and the pets who joined her there would be the catalyst for her appearance.

As I joined her in the Garden I would always learn something new. Such was the case of Joleen, one of the most caring and protective mother cats that would cross our path. On a wet and cold night a truck driver at a rest stop was startled by the sound of tiny meows emitting from the darkness of a trash dumpster. While many could have and possibly had already, turned a deaf ear to the calls of help that dark, damp night, he took the greater path and flashlight in hand began a search for the source. He would soon become a savior of sorts for a forgotten troupe of lost souls; he ultimately helped write several chapters in the book of life for many of us.

Abandoned in the grime and filth of what would have become their coffin were the shining eyes of three small kittens. Hiding among the trash, cups and fast food bags the little gray refugees resembled stained cotton balls. Only a good cleaning would reveal their true identity. As shocking and harsh as it was that someone could discard these small babies was the discovery of their mother. Holding her ground and ready to defend her litter, a matted, long haired, Lilac Point, Siamese protected her brood. Her eyes locked on the truck driver while she waited guardedly.

As the cry for help went out, more people showed up to observe and offer advice on the proper rescue techniques for three dirty kittens and an overly protective mother who had refused to abandon them to their fate. In short time a call to our rescue organization would be made. The situation explained, a call to volunteers and the wheels of our organization would begin to churn. Rescue members rushed to the rest stop where caring hands would gather up the mom and her babies. Some would refer to them as dirty, sick and beyond help. However, my wife, upon seeing them, simply referred to the kittens as "her own."

My wife, Alisa, the savior of anything small and furry, ignored the warnings about taking in the entire brood from some of the other rescue people and instead directed their recovery efforts. From the darkness of the dumpster they would come next to our house, where other rescue members, waiting with a sink full of soapy water and warm towels, would begin the process of cleansing the litter from their recent confinement.

Now I who love kittens above all else, decided after holding one of these babies, that I had never felt anything so disgusting in my life. If you had dipped a round ball of fur into a vat of chicken grease and fireplace soot, you would have a close idea of what they felt like. To make it worse, two, even three baths only touched the tip of the iceberg on these tiny creatures. Though I would announce to all who would listen that my hands would never touch these grease balls again, time would prove me a liar.

Over the next few weeks, these small babies, Josie, Jester and Jewel, would begin to grow into healthy, happy balls of energy. As their fur began to grow out, their protective mother, Joleen, continued to groom them until they took up the

In Heaven Kittens Play

task themselves. While Jewel would move in with my sister-in-law Elizabeth and Jester would find new digs with a rescue volunteer, both Joleen and Josie would stay with us.

As rescue parents, litters of "mousers", a term of cat endearment, often came and went... especially during "kitten" season. Joleen took it upon herself to play mom to most of these newly acquired orphans, treating them as if they were her own. She would groom them, nurse them and sleep among them as if she had birthed them, each and every one. Joleen proved to be a professional mother cat always pushing her way in to inspect the new arrivals, sniff noses, clean bottoms and often try to carry them off even as my wife was attending to them.

Then one evening we noticed that Joleen was missing. She had been under the weather for a few days, just acting as if she didn't feel well. At the time we lived in a huge two story house that provided all kinds of cubby holes and comfortable hideouts for kitties trying to fulfill their daily routine of eighteen hours sleep. We searched up and down, under every piece of furniture and in every nook and cranny with no luck. Then my wife finally found her, curled up in the rear of an open coat closet having died. She appeared to have simply laid down to take a nap and didn't wake up.

The little mother who had so valiantly protected her own kittens in a cold, dirty dumpster,
who had greeted, nursed and loved so many
motherless kittens in rescue had crossed over. She
would go to rest in our kitten peace garden out in
the old fruit orchard. A statue of a sleeping kitten
would come to mark her grave. It was an expression of Joleen's most important mission during
her life on earth, her devotion to protecting the
small and weak.

Two days after Joleen's death my wife would
lose a small rescue kitten to a respiratory infection.
The tiny Flame Point, just two or three weeks old
that had beaten the odds to have made it this far
had passed on that day. His journey to the Garden
would open up yet another chapter for me as I
received a visit from the Blue Angel that night.
Sitting on the ground the Blue Angel held the tiny
kitten on her lap, but my attention was immediately drawn to the figure of Joleen who paced
impatiently back and forth in front of her. Joleen
was quite fixed on the baby that the angel held.
Tail held high as she brushed and rubbed against
the angel, Joleen kept up a serenade of meows,
mirts and twirls. Every few laps standing up on
her back legs she would lean into the angel's lap to
sniff and bat gently at the kitten. Finally, with a
smile, the angel placed the kitten on the ground

near Joleen. As she began to groom the new arrival, the kitten looked at her without fear, his eyes bright and peaceful. Then to my surprise, Joleen, took the kitten by the scruff of its neck and began to carry it off into the brush near the angel. As she disappeared out of sight with the kitten hanging limply in her grasp, the angel grinned and standing up motioned for me to come with her. I followed as the angel strolled, arms crossed, in the direction Joleen had gone. Past trees and flowers the angel lead me, maybe a distance of fifty or so feet, where we came to a section of high grass and brush. The angel knelt down and with her arm, swept the grass aside to reveal a small grotto in a pile of rocks. Just inside the protection of the rocks, on a bed of leaves lay Joleen, her loud purrs filling the small space. His little paws kneading the stomach of his new mother, the little kitten, happily and safely nursed upon her.

"For Joleen," the angel said turning to me, "this is the desire of her heart, to protect and love kittens." For the next few moments, the angel explained that many mother cats miss the act of mothering kittens. Some long for their babies who died before they had the chance to grow. But it became immediately apparent that in His wisdom and hunger to see that all of His creations are happy, God had provided for Joleen and the kitten.

He had brought both together in heaven, and provided Joleen and other mothers like her, a chance to raise and love kittens without the interruption or fear of death or separation.

As we quietly left Joleen and the kitten, the angel explained that in the Garden of Pets, that animals never aged, with one exception. Kittens would continue to nurse and grow until they reached the age, where on earth, they would have survived on their own. "But why," I asked the angel. The answer was simply because God wanted them to grow to the age that they could play, chase and enjoy life. "A baby kitten," she explained, "if they never aged, would not experience these joys, all they would ever know is sleeping and that was not in God's plan for his creations."

During my visits to the Garden I often see Joleen resting or walking close to the Blue Angel. In death, much as she did in life, Joleen enjoys the company of people. So many times as I've witnessed her in the Garden she has had a kitten in tow, proudly parading her charge around for everyone to see, always with a twinkle of happiness in her eyes.

The Lord had given Joleen the desire of her heart, being a mom and mothering kittens, happily serving her special role in heaven just as she did in life.

* * * * *

Nighttime in the Garden of Pets is both different and special. The sun-like glow begins to fade until a twilight envelopes the Garden. Everywhere the animals curl up to sleep, some alone, many entwined with another playmate. Mothers gather their babies close to them and even the angels lay and close their eyes to dream.

During this time God quietly enters the Garden. Like a breeze He moves to touch and bless each and every soul who rests there. The Creator gently snuggles every creature within His protective arms. Babies gaze lovingly through newborn eyes upon His face, others purr with pleasure as their paws happily kneed He who holds them.

Lastly Father God goes to each and every angel and holds them close. He softly praises them for their devotion to the creatures He made and loves. Then like a breeze He is gone to visit another of His gardens.

The Garden is a quiet scene of tranquility. Kittens slumber, babies peacefully nurse their mothers and the angels dream.

Nick L. Sacco

"Are we really sure the purring is coming from the kitty and not from our very own hearts?"

- Terri Guillemets

Chapter Five

Reborn

In our many years working in rescue we saw cats of every size, color and temperament. While most come to us with all their body parts intact, some, through illness or accident did not. One eye or ear, missing a limb, a half or no tail at all. These imperfections didn't mean a forever home wasn't waiting for them.

Indiana Jones, our sleek, one-eyed Abyssinian, belonged to such ranks. Kansas City Siamese Rescue liberated Indy from an inhumane kitty mill operation. His breeders looked upon him as damaged goods because he had lost an eye to infection and was sickly. They were going to destroy him when the group learned about his situation.

Indiana, who always looked for the highest point in any room, had selected the top of our refrigerator as his observation point and private lounging area. His love for high and perilous places concerned me, especially when he would place all four of his paws on the edge of the refrigerator, lean forward in a gravity defying manner and stare at the rotating ceiling fan. His body would tense up like a high tension spring as he pondered attempting the feat.

From this perch, he could observe everyone and everything who entered his domain and would greet them with a welcoming meow. Indiana Jones was smart. He had deduced that the food lived in the kitchen, therefore, if one of the "peoples" came into the kitchen, probability had it their visit involved something good to eat. Indy knew that if he put on his best "charming" act, then whatever family member was roaming around his kitchen likely would share. While he enjoyed wet cat food he preferred cold cuts, cheese and other human foods that came in cans or wrapped in plastic. From his perch, Indy was the Master of all he saw which included the stovetop, microwave and can opener.

Despite operating with only one eye his depth of field did not seem to be affected. Indiana Jones would lock his eye on us the moment we entered the kitchen. Standing at the edge of the fridge, he would judge the distance between us, do a quick check of wind speed and direction, and then suddenly launch himself into mid-air. It didn't matter if you were two feet or six feet away. With the agility of a mountain goat he would kick off with his muscular legs and soar through the air to complete a three-point landing on your shoulder. He would perform this feat as if he had done it a thousand times before and now that I think about it, he probably had. His touchdowns were beautiful, carried out with text-book precision, remarkably soft and gentle. Indiana never put out a nail upon landing. Some cats feel an obligation to secure their hold. This involves drastic and painful methods. They are the ones who hit you spread eagle, their paws wide open, and nails extended like bayonets. Indiana would signal the conclusion of his gymnastic event with a solid head butt into your cheek and a cold nose on your neck.

After about four years we lost Indiana to kidney failure. He went over very peacefully with the gentle help of our favorite veterinarian, Dr. Laura. We loved our vet from day one. Laura is a tall, thin woman with short, red hair who can crack a joke one minute and then become professional and serious the next. We always felt comfortable with her and her medical advice. While we had to spend many sad times together, gathered around an exam table as she ended the suffering of a beloved pet, we also drew strength from her support and professionalism.

The night of Indiana's death I drifted off to sleep and quickly found myself standing in the beauty of the Garden. As I offered a quick greeting to the Blue Angel who walked towards me, arms crossed and smiling, I detected the familiar sounds of Indy nearby but could not see him. I looked toward the angel hoping for guidance from her. Without saying a word or moving, she smiled at me, raised her eyes upwards as if to say, "look there." I absorbed the angel's tip and turning my face towards the sky, spotted Indiana Jones pacing back and forth on a tree limb I guessed to be five feet above me.

When I first saw Indy it took a moment for me to realize this beautiful animal was actually him. First he appeared much younger, his coat shiny and clean and his eyes, sparkling. Yes, Indy the amazing one-eyed cat no longer looked like a pirate. The angel moved closer to me and held her arms upwards towards her new tree dweller. Just like Indiana Jones had done hundreds of times in our kitchen, he leapt with perfect grace to land upon the shoulders of his guardian angel.

It immediately occurred to me that Indy had made no effort to come to me. But I had noticed this before during visits. While nothing had ever been said to me, somehow I knew that while granted the privilege of coming into the Garden, I

was not a member of this special club. While I could watch and speak with the angel and her charges, to hold and love these animals was a special entitlement that only the Blue Angel was allowed.

As I looked at the beautiful Indiana Jones, standing proudly upon the angel's shoulders, I recalled the promise made to us in the Bible that a new body, free of sickness and imperfection awaited us. Indiana Jones confirmed this wonderful assurance as he sat upon the angel's shoulder, smiling at me with his two, beautiful, bright green eyes.

Nick L. Sacco

*"I believe cats to be spirits come to earth.
A cat, I am sure, could walk on a cloud
without coming through."*

- Jules Verne

Chapter Six

More Gifts

Another such example of this gift was also shared with me. It involved a younger kitten that came into rescue and who for a short time claimed our house as her home. Like so many others, she had come to us already fighting illness and malnourishment. We named her Crystal, a beautiful, solid white, short hair with deep blue eyes, she quickly established herself as an accomplished lap cat. She was one of those who appeared out of thin air whenever your behind hit a chair or you flopped down on a couch. Purring her own monologue during the evening news, Price Is Right or a movie, she was quite content to keep a lap warm, and of course, inspect the snack du jour.

After succumbing to illness, I was summoned to the Garden. I wasn't quite sure why, as this kitten had only graced us for a short time. Although I enjoyed her company I did not claim her as a furry soul mate befitting a special visit. Upon seeing the Blue Angel, something appeared to be wrong, something I had not experienced in my prior visits with the Blue Angel. All I could see of Crystal was her small head peeking out from under the folds of the angel's robe. The angel, who I had learned was named Sarah, sat calmly upon a log, slightly leaning forward, arms crossed, an impish grin on her face. But something was wrong with Crystal, as it was obvious she appeared scared and uncertain. As usual, the area around the angel was a beehive of activity. While some lounged lazily in the soft grass, others raced at breakneck "cat dash" speed back and forth near the angel. Joleen, a kitten in tow, approached and offered a mirt and trill of welcome to the new arrival. Crystal, however, quickly vanished back under the folds of the angel's robes, her nose and eyes only to reappear a moment later.

The angel, still hosting her grin and detecting my concern with Crystal's behavior, reached down and lifted her out from within the robe. Holding her close to her face the angel placed her lips against Crystal's ear and began to whisper. Immediately Crystal reacted with a quick shake of her head, and then leaned forward to touch her nose to the angel's lips. "This kitten," the angel said, looking towards me holding cheek to cheek with Crystal, "has never heard sound before. This is a totally new experience for her."

It all became clear. I had forgotten that Crystal was deaf from birth, a genetic abnormality often found in solid white cats with blue eyes. With her new body came the ability to hear, which created uncertainty of her new sensory experience. "She has never heard the birds, the wind or another kitten talking," the angel explained, still holding Crystal close. "In a short time," Sarah said, "she will embrace her new gift and her fear will vanish."

Thus another lesson learned from the Blue Angel. In an illustration involving a small white cat experiencing sound for the first time, I came to realize that each of us, in heaven, will leave our worn and damaged bodies at death's door and step into something perfect, flawless and beautiful.

"There are two means of refuge from the miseries of life: music and cats."

- Albert Schweitzer

Chapter Seven

Transformation

To this day Thomas O'Mally holds a special place in our lives, and in more ways than one. He was a huge Flame Point Ragdoll stray who had become a fast food restaurant "dumpster diver." He was rescued, and came to live with us. Like anyone who has survived by scrounging through someone else's garbage, O'Mally came to us smelling like a piece of burnt toast wrapped around a dead fish. To make matters worse, Thomas O'Mally maintained the plumbing of an old tomcat and was happy to share his aroma of manhood with all those with which he came into contact.

In a short time, Thomas received a trip through the kitty carwash followed by a "stop and snip" visit to the vet. Even though my wife told O'Mally as she drove him to the animal hospital, that he was there for a day spa, he would quickly learn the true purpose of this vacation.

In Heaven Kittens Play

But, being the most loving cat that had come into our part of the rescue operation, Thomas quickly forgave and forgot and was happy to live in the kennel with several other refugees.

At that time, our kennel was located in an old, stone barn just behind our house in the fruit orchard. Concrete floor, lots of windows, sunlight, breeze and room to run made this a perfect place for a cat to live. Just outside the windows there was always a flurry of activity. Birds constantly kept coming and going from the feeders there. In addition a small army of squirrels would calmly sit three inches outside the chicken wire, oblivious to the tail swishing, wannabe predators, staring at them.

Yes, Thomas O'Mally ran a tight ship out in the barn. Crickets, grasshoppers, spiders or other various forms of creepy crawlers who dared violate the sovereignty of the kennel were subject to swift and severe punishment. Apparently, the snake missed the memo. One summer day, my wife had gone into the barn to feed and water. As she entered the barn she was shocked first at the sight of blood sprayed across the floor, and next, the figure of a long black snake laying motionless in the center of the room. Her first concern was that the blood belonged to that of one of the cats. Then she saw Thomas O'Mally. Laying happily on his back mere inches from the deceased reptile, the huge Thomas O'Mally, who tipped the scale at an easy fifteen pounds, rolled contently, basking in his victory over the now dead serpent. Yes, Thomas O'Mally, ruler of the kennel had reinforced the fact that anything entering the barn without invitation would become "entertainment."

While Thomas took offense to other creatures coming into the barn, including fellow cats, O'Mally loved people. This was true whether he was rubbing up against your legs, zigzagging between your feet as you walked, or hopping from window seat to window seat until he was next to you. Thomas would lay in your arms as long as you would hold him. Curled up purring contently, Thomas had used this method to win the heart of my wife. While in the barn performing her rescue chores, she would carry on a conversation with O'Mally about him finding a forever home. She would tell him stories of warm houses and loving families. Thomas would listen intently, holding his tail high and meowing his approval.

Then suddenly, with little warning, O'Mally began to fail. He was taken to Doctor Laura, who diagnosed him with a serious infection. Medical treatment began, antibiotics were given but O'Mally continued his decline. He went downhill so quickly that he was soon placed in a "sick cage" where my wife could treat him. The sick cage was one of those shiny, sanitary, aluminum enclosures that screamed vet's office. O'Mally had, for nearly three months, shared his love with all people and had probably consumed his body weight in grasshoppers and spiders. Now he could barely hold his head up when someone entered the room.

Nothing was working. A number of medicines were tried, IV's began, fluids given. My wife struggled to get him to eat but O'Mally, despite her best life saving efforts, quietly passed away.

So ill had he gotten, the once healthy and shiny O'Mally had become a shell of his former self. His sickness had robbed him of his beauty, leaving in its place a gaunt, thin casualty of disease. As so many cats do when they become ill, Thomas had ceased grooming himself several days before his death. As a result, his long shiny fur had become dull, matted and dirty. His handsome muzzle was caked with days of dried mucous from his nose and the remains of numerous failed forced feedings.

In my past visits with the Blue Angel, I was accustomed to seeing cats and kittens who had passed over. While some sat on her lap, lounged or played nearby, all were reborn when I saw them. Thomas O'Mally was the exception. As the scene appeared before me, the Blue Angel sat quietly holding the loathsome, dead body of O'Mally on her lap. A feeling of sadness came over me as I stared at the depressing and discouraging scene in front of me.

But then I saw a look in the angel's eyes. They twinkled and a smile on her lips seemed to say, "Wait and watch." As she lowered her eyes downwards to O'Mally's body, I did as well and observed the most wonderful miracle of my life. It started slowly and silently. Beginning at the very tip of Thomas O'Mally's tail, it was as if a gentle breeze began to blow. Yet the leaves on the ground and the material of the angel's robe and her own strands of hair remained motionless. In the twinkle of an eye this unseen gust of air began to travel across O'Mally's fur. As it did I could see the dirty fur being lifted up as if an invisible hand was brushing across it. But to my amazement, as the strands of hair fell back into place they had been transformed clean, pristine and new.

As the breeze flowed across his body it gently stroked his ears, tweaked his whiskers and caused his eyelids to flutter. In a beautiful sight which I will never, ever forget, I saw the most wonderful transformation take place. Where a sad, lifeless cat once lay, now, O'Mally, younger and reborn raised his head and calmly viewed the world around him.

At first, O'Mally just sat up and like any cat who had just awoken from a nap performed a perfect cat stretch, tail arched upwards, head down and front legs extended. But then, as he rose on all fours, he turned locking his eyes on the angel's face. Thomas O'Mally turned towards the Blue Angel, placed his front paws around her neck, and ever-so-gently lowered his head onto the angel's shoulder and began to hug her. The angel contently returned the show of affection and love, drawing the new O'Mally into her arms as they silently held one another.

*"Who can believe that there is
no soul behind those luminous eyes!"*

- Theophile Gautier

Chapter Eight

Guardians

Over the years and after so many wonderful visits with the Blue Angel, I've been witness to and learned much about the Garden of Pets.

It has surprised me that most people, when learning the story of the Blue Angel, show a spark of interest to learn more. Like me they express a feeling of comfort knowing about the Blue Angel and her garden. Several contact me inquiring about a beloved pet who has passed on. Occasionally I am asked if I know why the angel appeared to me. As I have said, I am not an expert on angels but on a sad night that I laid with a dying kitten, I prayed and asked questions in the most heartfelt manner and God answered.

When I first met Sarah, the Blue Angel, she identified herself as a "Guardian Angel," which prompted me to ask where were her wings? I'd seen religious pictures, watched movies and spent years in Catholic school. That was back in the olden days when the nuns wore the entire black and white habit and carried a wooden ruler in a shoulder holster. Why didn't the angel sport a flowing pair of wings?

The answer I would receive is that there are two types of angels. The first, are "Celestial" angels or winged angels. These are a higher form of angel who have never lived an earthbound life. They were created in the Beginning and have always existed with God. Sarah, however, is one of the second class and is a Guardian Angel, someone who was born and lived a human life at one time. These angels have, by their own choice, chosen to return to earth to protect someone, to teach, comfort, guide and perform miracles. Others, like Sarah, desired to become guardians of their own pet and animal-filled garden.

What she said, immediately and clearly, made all the sense in the world to me. What a wonderful gift after we leave this world to be offered the opportunity to accept such a special role, to protect, teach or love animals.

During this meeting, Sarah said to me, "I have been granted permission to answer your questions." This statement made me feel that I had asked God for a request and it had been answered. Does that mean that the Blue Angel answers every mystery of the Bible, can give me the winning lottery numbers or share with me the answer of what really happened to Jimmy Hoffa or Amelia Earhart? No. The angel shares with me exactly what I had asked for. What happens to pets and animals when they die?

Sarah reassured me that there are countless Gardens of Pets, some attended by a single angel and some with two or more guardians. Some contain orphaned pets who never knew the love and tenderness of a human being. Whether they died as babies or lived a short life alone struggling to survive, there is a Garden waiting for them and an angel eager to show them the love they have missed.

"Your cat will never threaten your popularity by barking at three in the morning. He won't attack the mailman or eat the drapes, although he may climb the drapes to see how the room looks from the ceiling."

- Helen Powers

Chapter Nine

Dad

In 2004 my wife returned from the animal clinic with a bounce in her step and a twinkle in her eye. While there she had met "Tommy," a young, beautiful Golden Retriever who had been found wandering loose in a nice area of Kansas City. Despite signs being posted and word passed about, Tommy went unclaimed for several weeks.

Friendly and loving, Tommy had the most wonderful and gentle personality of any dog I had met. With a red, shiny coat and sparkling eyes he had shmoozed my wife at the vet's office. The vet, apparently in cahoots with Tommy, made my wife an offer. If she would simply pay the vet bill, Tommy was hers. The vet and my wife spit in the palms of their hands, shook on the deal and we suddenly had a new dog.

Tommy immediately made himself at home in our family. He loved the farm and whether he was in the orchard, garden or racing through the waist-high grass of the fields, Tommy never went far. Tommy loved the pond in our backyard which was filled with goldfish, brightly colored Japanese Koi and tropical plants, Tommy decided that this body of water was to be his own play area. Often times he would sit at the edge, lapping at the water and snapping at fish who swam just inches around him. Other times, there would be a flash of red fur and a splash as Tommy would launch himself into the center of the pond. He would happily wade around the pond while a small entourage of fish zipped back and forth around him. Dripping wet, he would climb from the pond, violently shake his body sending water droplets flying in every direction. He'd then race for the backdoor and wait to be allowed inside so he could share his wet dog smell with my wife's favorite couch.

Tommy loved the farm, the pond and oh yes, our cats. About the time that Tommy came to live with us my wife had received a young little kitten by the name of "Bing." Like so many before him, Bing, a cute little Seal Point Siamese, came to us sick. While my wife nursed him back to health with various medicines she also began to feed him with a baby bottle. Tommy quickly learned that this new kitty tasted good and began a ritual of cleaning Bing's face after every feeding. Tommy and Bing bonded together and as the kitten grew larger the two of them became close friends. It was not uncommon to find the two of them curled up asleep together or playing with one another.

But a day would come when Tommy would disappear. For as long as Tommy had lived with us he never strayed far from the house. Normally just yelling his name from the back porch would bring the big goof running at a gallop from the back forty. This changed when one day we received a young, rescue pup. While the two got along well, we noticed that when we let them out and called for them to return it took longer and longer for them to find their way back home. With all of the acreage it wasn't out of the norm for them to be near the back fence somewhere. With all the rabbits and squirrels and other wildlife that inhabited our property I figured Tommy was teaching the new pup the fine art of hunting and the pleasure of bringing something furry and dead back to the house to share with my screaming wife.

One day the two didn't return. A thorough search of the garden, orchard and fields turned up nothing. We drove down the streets and around the neighborhood without any sign of them. They had disappeared into thin air. Then after a day of them missing I climbed the fence at the far edge of our property. A short walk, picking yourself through the barbs and branches led to a drop off of about twenty-five feet. At the bottom ran a set of train tracks. I scrambled, almost sliding down the steep dirt incline to reach the bottom. Standing up and dusting myself off I let my eyes glance down the track's steel rails and immediately spotted what I had feared most.

After Tommy was laid to rest in our pet garden in the orchard I conducted a check of the fence line. I would discover that a large tree in the back had apparently fallen down during a wind or thunderstorm, smashing the fence and creating an opening. While Tommy never left his property, we suspect that the new pup found the broken fence and made his way out with Tommy following, as dogs are known to do. Or, for all we know it could have been the other way around. Either way, good old Tommy had left us for better digs.

Within the week I received an invitation to the Blue Angel's garden. As usual I made a point to spot who was around and what they were doing. Joleen our motherly cat was proudly pacing around with a new kitten right beside her, others lounged lazily in the grass and a couple of young kittens wrestled and pounced on one another in the bushes near myself and the angel. Laying, paws crossed besides the Blue Angel was a very beautiful and bright-eyed Tommy. He looked at me, eyes smiling and tail wagging, but made no move to get up or approach. It was then I truly came to the realization that while I've been blessed with visits to the Blue Angel's garden I was really not a part of it. I can communicate and see those wonderful animals who live with her but an invisible line is drawn. In this spiritual plane the earthbound and the reborn can't make contact. If so, I'd have had seventy-five pounds of Golden Retriever up in my arms licking my face.

Then something to the left caught my eye. In the distance, walking through the fields towards us appeared a figure. Someone or something was with it. The Blue Angel stood, gently stroking a Calico cat in her arms looking out at the same approaching shapes. As I continued to watch the figures became more clear, it was a man, that was sure, and what seemed to be a dog beside him. Carefully I watched the man steadily walk towards us, his arms swinging at his sides. Glancing at the Blue Angel's feet, Tommy had also spotted them and was now sitting up, his tail beating a swath in the grass below him. However, it was the figure approaching us that had Tommy all excited. He suddenly jumped up on all fours, his entire body swinging happily in rhythm with his tail.

I returned my gaze to the approaching figures. I looked more closely. Something about the way the man walked and carried himself was familiar.

Slowly, as if awakening from a dream it became clear. I felt a leap in my heart just as Tommy ran forward to greet him. It was my father, who had passed away in 1992. As Tommy bounded forward in delight I saw that the dog trotting beside him was the reptile hunting Lucky of my youth. Both dogs greeted one another as if best of friends, jumping on one another as wrestling dogs do. Tails waving and tongues rolling.

There is some disagreement about my father's origins. For years I thought he had been born in Sicily and came over with his mother and brothers as an infant. Later we would learn he was born in St. Louis and raised in the Italian section known as "The Hill." Either way, Dad was raised in a very Sicilian household and spoke nothing but Italian until he was in the third grade. He was a stocky built, hard working man with strong Italian features, who wasn't happy if he wasn't doing something. For years, even in illness, he was a fit guy with little or no fat on him, a veteran of the great depression, who knew what it was to do without and to be hungry. While Dad, himself, wasn't in the Italian mob that didn't mean he wasn't "connected." I grew up watching him visit with lots of other Italian men, who I might say, were self employed.

But now I found myself staring at my father as I knew him from younger photographs, a full head of dark hair, muscular, thin frame but still wearing his trademark short-sleeved white shirt and dark slacks. As my dad and the angel greeted one another with a warm and lingering hug, the angel placed the kitten upon the ground. Then releasing his hold on the Blue Angel, Dad turned his attention to Tommy. Kneeling down he reached to pull the big, red dog to him.

For reasons that I can't explain I felt a need to give my father a warning. "Don't worry, Dad," I suddenly said, "Tommy's a good dog." At this point Tommy had fallen on his side, smiling and rolling in the leaves presenting his stomach should Dad so choose to rub it. Looking up at me with a warm smile, Dad replied, "I know Tommy's a good dog son. That's why I'm here. I'm here for Tommy."

With that he stood up and patted his leg with the universal dog message of "come here". Turning he began to walk back the way he had come, however, now Tommy and Lucky led the way, running side by side as if friends forever. Slowly the three of them became smaller and smaller until out of sight, as the angel and I silently watched them go.

Why had Dad come for Tommy, I asked myself. I thought about it for a while and realized there were two reasons. One is the fact that Dad loved big dogs. The second is because Tommy held such a place of importance in the hearts of myself and especially my wife, Alisa. To me, Dad came to take Tommy to be with him until myself or Alisa made the journey over.

Nick L. Sacco

"Most of us rather like our cats to have a streak of wickedness. I should not feel quite easy in the company of any cat that walked about the house with a saintly expression."

- Beverly Nichols

Chapter Ten

Rescue

I've learned over the years that the volunteers who work in animal rescue are a special type of individual. Most people's first and only experience with a rescue person is when they meet them at a local adoption event. It's usually a busy and loud atmosphere. Dogs barking, cats meowing, people shuffling around as if they were all in a narrow hallway. Volunteers lifting a new kitten into a little girl's waiting arms, others vying for position to peek into a cage at the patient, loving face gazing back at them.

What's not seen is all the work the volunteers perform behind the scenes. Contrary to popular belief, not every rescue group has a sparkling, state-of-the art animal kennel staffed with veterinarians and support people. In fact most animal rescue people keep the fosters within their own homes. Cats and dogs may come and go depending on the success of their adoption events, however, there is never a day a rescue volunteer fears their home will be empty. Constantly new furry children come to live with them. Some given up by their owners and some strays. But the volunteer is always ready to feed, clean up after, transport back and forth from the vet's office and of course, to love them, the short or long time they remain a temporary part of their family.

A true volunteer will spend their own time and money for these babies who need them, sometimes driving states away to pick someone up or to place a pet in the hands of their new mother or father. Many a time we've pulled into the parking lot of a convenience store to be greeted by a family waiting eagerly outside their minivan like we were Santa just arrived.

Rescue people will not shy away from taking another pet even though their spouse has already been screaming and beating their chest about the ever increasing number of pets in the home. They will learn to pill even the most resistant feline without batting an eye, become an expert at giving a shot, spotting ringworm, an infection or even something worse and then acting upon it. Often times they more closely resemble a type of animal paramedic or ER nurse.

Animal rescue men and women will be there in the bad and the good. They will celebrate the birth of helpless newborns and plan for the future. They will also be there at the end, holding a pet during their final minutes, feeling sad and often shedding tears for an animal who has been with them only a short time.

"It is impossible for a lover of cats to banish these alert, gentle, and discriminating little friends, who give us just enough of their regard and complaisance to make us hunger for more."

- Agnes Repplier

Chapter Eleven

The Ride

Anyone who is owned by a cat knows the dread associated with keeping their litter box clean and acceptable to their standards. Slack in your duties and you'll find they will leave you a nice little reminder that you're failing in your duties; ergo, a little present outside the litter box, in your bathtub or even in your house shoe. Litter boxes are a sacred place to a kitty and you are expected to maintain its pristine condition.

A day came that we introduced our kitty herd to a new device, one of those automatic litter boxes, the ones that sense when the cat has done his business and then left. A rake at one end then sweeps the litter and deposits the waste in a plastic container to dispose of later.

We read the directions, installed the new device, filled it with litter, plugged it into the closest socket and waited. The cats ignored it. My wife tried to lure them in with her baby-like kitty talk. No luck. One old Siamese stuck his head in the door just long enough to give the new litter box an ugly look and a stare before leaving in a huff. The new, fancy, state-of-the-art poop scooper was not receiving a warm welcome.

As cat lovers know, during a traditional litter box scooping, cats often enter the box before you've had the opportunity to complete the maintenance. Thus, disinterest from the cats was unanticipated. It was decided we would simply leave it be and give the cats a chance to become accustomed to it.

Several hours would go by until, to our surprise, we could hear the new box down the hall churning through the slightly noisy cycle of cleaning. Like little kids on Christmas morning we ran down the hall to see the device in operation. Upon arrival the bathroom was empty, whomever had triggered it was long gone. However, it had been used and Alisa and I did the happy dance that we hadn't wasted a large amount of money on something the cats would shun like the plague.

Later in the evening, sitting in our recliners watching television, we would smile at one another when we heard the whirring of the new litter box. As the evening progressed the activity from the bathroom became more frequent. The time between cycles began to shorten from every thirty minutes, to fifteen minutes then five and finally as quickly as one cycle ended another would begin.

Alisa gave me her "Oh crap something's wrong," look and quietly we crept down the hall until we stood on opposite sides of the bathroom door and cautiously peeked in. I will never forget the scene that awaited us. All the cats were sitting in a circle around the new litter box, very intently watching it. As soon as it finished its cleaning cycle and the rake part returned to its home base, one of the waiting cats would step into it, scratch around, do their business, scratch some more like a burying cat does, and then retake their observation position with the others. As the automatic litter box sensed the cat was gone it would, again, begin its cleaning duties. As the rake moved through the clumping litter all eyes were fixed on it.

Alisa and I stood there speechless watching the show in front of us. To make matters worse, we had a seven-week-old Calico kitten named Tweenke who was in on the show. Tweenke, however, was actually sitting on top of the arm that controlled the rake mechanism. As the arm moved from the beginning position down the length of the litter box, Tweenke sat perched calmly, riding the arm back and forth as the other cats looked on.

It came as no surprise to us that the new, automatic litter box's days were already numbered. Within ten days it would die completely, I'm certain in our home it had been used extensively more than the design engineers ever planned for.

Receipt in hand we returned it to Walmart. The clerk pleasantly asked us if we wanted to exchange it. We answered in unison..."NO!" We wanted a traditional litter box, not an amusement ride.

"No heaven will not ever Heaven be
Unless my cats are there to welcome me."

- Author Unknown

Chapter Twelve

Lazarus

People who look at animal rescue from the outside don't really understand that all is not happy and cheerful. They may pass an animal rescue tent at an event or inside their local animal shelter and feel their heart jump. The cute faces of puppies greeting everyone who near their cage. Tongues hanging out, tails wagging and an ambience sound of barks and growls. Young kittens reach through cage bars to bat playfully at a human finger extended to them. Couples will hold and fawn over a dog or cat in their arms as they make the decision to take them home. An animal rescue event often creates a carnival air.

Behind the scenes, however, animal rescue volunteers spend many hours dealing with sick pets. A cold, infection, and often worse. Such was the case of the cat named Lazarus. First, Lazarus' real name was Clyde and he had come, kicking and screaming, into rescue.

Clyde, obviously homeless, had begun dumpster diving in the trash behind the Wendy's restaurant. Employees taken with his shiny black fur and sparkling blue eyes had begun feeding their new visitor. As winter was nearing it was decided that Clyde would be taken in by one of the employees and turned over to rescue. Clyde, however, had different plans and being caught by someone in an apron and paper hat wasn't one of them. After several failed attempts to lure him close enough for capture a call was made to our rescue team.

By the time a team of rescuers arrived at the Wendy's, live trap in hand, the employees had noticed Clyde apparently beginning to feel ill. The trap was baited and left. Over the next three days two opossums, five raccoons and a handful of neighborhood cats were caught but Clyde remained free. Then one night an employee emptying trash discovered Clyde, laying listless behind the restaurant. The first volunteer on the scene easily scooped him up and Clyde began his journey into rescue.

Clyde came to live in a sick cage in our basement where my wife, Alisa, began to treat him with the medicine and methods that she had. When no improvement was made a trip, then two, were made to the local vet's office.

Doctor Laura pulled no punches when it came to the condition of an animal. If she thought there was hope to be had she would present the options. But if the diagnosis was grim she would lay it on the line. Examining Clyde in a tender, yet professional manner, Doctor Laura determined that Clyde was suffering from a very serious respiratory infection and considering he'd lived outdoors for several weeks, she gave him very little chance of survival. He was dosed with penicillin and brought back home to his sick cage where he lay unmoving.

The following morning as I was returning from working the night shift, my wife notified me that she had found Clyde dead that morning. She had placed his body in a carrier in the garage and asked that I take him to the vet's office for disposal when I awoke later in the afternoon.

Around 2 pm in the afternoon I arose and headed to the garage to fulfill my duty. As I entered the basement I felt I should be ringing a bell and yelling, "Bring out your dead." It was far from the first time I had transported a dead animal to the vet but I still dreaded it.

Pulling my car keys from my pocket and clicking the garage button on the wall I decided a quick detour was in store to bring the empty trash cans up from the end of the drive to avoid accidentally backing over them. As I placed them inside the garage a loud meow greeted me. I scanned the floor around me to make sure one of our own pets hadn't followed me outside. Again a loud meow echoed around the garage. Turning I looked towards the far garage door where a medium-sized carrier sat. Inside, sitting straight and alert, Clyde calmly stared at me as he let out with another greeting.

I quickly looked around to make sure I wasn't missing the carrier my wife had told me about. Clyde was now rubbing contently against the inside of the cage door, tail held high while I quickly dialed my wife on my cell phone. A moment later she answered from her office phone.

"Where's this dead cat," I asked.

"He's in the carrier in the garage," she replied.

Wanting to make sure I was understanding correctly I asked, "We are speaking about Clyde, he's in the brown carrier in the garage and he's dead...right?"

"Yes," Alisa replied, "he was dead when I checked on him this morning".

"Well he's not dead anymore," I explained calmly. "He's bouncing around his carrier like a yo-yo. I even stuck a finger in and touched him to make sure I wasn't dreaming," I told her.

There was a long pause as Alisa took in the news. "Look," I told her, "I'm putting your dead cat back inside the house. I realize that I'm not a trained animal doctor or anything, however, I do know a live cat from a dead cat and Clyde is most definitely not dead".

Moments later a very happy Clyde snuggled up in my arms and I took him inside where he promptly gobbled down an entire can of soft food by himself, washing it down with a long drink of fresh water.

As I watched him eat I just shook my head. "So tell me Lazarus," I jokingly asked him, "did you see the white light?"

Alisa would return that afternoon to find the formerly dead cat very intently grooming himself. "I swear he was cold and still when I woke up," she said.

Whatever had happened with Clyde I'm not sure. But he was no longer near death or even sick. A week later he would attend a mobile adoption event where a military family from Fort Leavenworth, Kansas fell in love with him. Their three children took turns holding the content, purring Clyde in their arms. He would leave that day with them and the children packed with armloads of new toys, food and litter to accompany him to his new home.

Lazarus was joining the army.

Nick L. Sacco

"Another cat? Perhaps. For love there is also a season; its seeds must be re-sown. But a family cat is not replaceable like a worn out coat or a set of tires. Each new kitten becomes its own cat, and none is repeated. I am four cats old, measuring out my life in friends that have succeeded but not replaced one another."

- Irving Townsend

Chapter Thirteen

Endings and Beginnings

My wife Alisa's love for animals began at a very young age. Growing up on a farm in rural Ray County, Missouri, she was accustomed to every type of animal, tame and wild that might take up residence there. Baby chickens given as an Easter present, would turn into mean roosters. After chasing Alisa up a tree they would eventually wind up on the dinner table courtesy of her grandmother. An entourage of beagles and dachshunds would accompany her on forays to the barn, ponds and fields. She would learn to ride horses at a young age while most of us were peddling our first bicycle.

Her older brother Charlie told of Alisa's need to care for others. "She was a nursemaid to sick puppies and a midwife to pregnant cats," he said. Alisa once told her mother that she wanted to grow up and have a cat farm. Clearly her dream, in many respects, came to be.

In 2000 Alisa came into contact with "Kansas City Siamese Rescue" after our youngest daughter, Kalli, found a cat on their web site. A trip down a dusty country road to their orphanage in an old barn, much as Alisa had grown up with, would lay the groundwork for her joining a group that would give her the pleasure and satisfaction of working with animals. It would also lead her into lifelong friendships.

Over a period of nine years Alisa would submerge herself into the efforts of this group. She would attend countless events and speak with thousands of people in her mission to match the right people with the right cat or kitten. She drove thousands of miles delivering cats to new homes and picking up mothers with their litters of newborns at local shelters. The ring of her phone was nearly always a call for help. Alisa, it seemed, had boundless energy when a tractor trailer of cat food or litter had to be unloaded or the kennel had to be cleaned.

She was known to kidnap female cats wandering the neighborhood looking for another Tom to impregnate them. They would mysteriously return to their homes and irresponsible owners a day or two later, their bellies shaved and a small scar to show their kitten rearing days were over.

But the most important gift that Alisa brought to animal rescue was her profound need to heal. This same trait is what led her to a life of serving others as a Registered Nurse. So many cats and kittens owe their lives to the efforts Alisa gave them. She intuitively picked up on the signs and symptoms of a sick animal and knew what to do, be it an injection, a certain medication and often a trip to the vets for more intense treatment. She would get up in the night to treat one of her sickies and often walked the floor in the dark quiet, a sick or slowly recovering kitten wrapped in her arms. Often times they stared quietly up at her with eyes soft and tender and I truly believe they understood the good and protective person who held them.

Despite her best efforts death often came to visit and each loss brought to her a certain sadness. I would find her standing in a special garden in the orchard of our farm pulling weeds around the many small statues and markers that dotted the ground and signified where a kitten rested.

In February of 2005 Alisa first acknowledged a lump in her left breast. A biopsy a few days later would bring the dark news that it was a very aggressive cancer. Alisa, ironically enough, had been a cancer nurse for over 25 years. Treating those suffering from this type of illness was what she did, not what she wanted to receive.

She would undergo a double mastectomy, weeks of radiation and months of chemotherapy. While the spread of the illness would be slowed it would never be stopped. While the cancer surged throughout her body she would continue to work diligently for the welfare of the rescue group and the kittens in their care, serving as President.

Eventually her health would decline to where she could no longer volunteer. Her days of actively rescuing and adopting homeless cats and kittens would end. Often times her friends in rescue would invite her to a Saturday adoption event. She would sit among her fellow volunteers happy to be even a small part of the event. Later a friend would phone reporting that Alisa was tired and I would drive to pick her up. As I helped her in the car I couldn't help but notice her sense of sadness as to how her life was shifting.

Alisa knew the end was near and that I could no longer care for both Alisa and the pets. Even as she suffered through the end stages of her cancer her thoughts were on both her personal cats and the few foster animals that remained in our care. Sitting with her head covered in a pink bandana, a blanket across her lap she scribbled upon a legal pad. She began to match up her cats with an "A List" of prior adopters and rescue volunteers. For the next few days Alisa would telephone or e-mail until she had matched her babies with suitable adopters. Leaving no loose ends she could now rest knowing her kittens were in good hands.

In March of 2010 Alisa's condition took a rapid turn for the worse. A day would come when her oncologist, Doctor Carol Fabian, would tearfully deliver the news that Alisa's days on this Earth were now measured in just weeks. Entering April, Alisa was spending more time hospitalized than home as the cancer quickly spread. One quiet night as I sat holding her hand at the hospital she said with tearful eyes how much she missed her kittens at home and wished they were with her.

An ambulance brought her back to her home for the final time on Friday, April 16th. Weak but comfortable in her own bed the animals she loved so much came to lay with her. Charlie Brown and Bing her Seal Point Siamese took up positions on her lap and stomach. Stella and Silhouette, her red and black Cornish Rex tunneled their way under her covers to lay beside her. For the rest of the day, in between friends and family coming to say goodbye, Alisa held court with her furry friends. She spoke quietly to Charlie Brown and Bing about what small, sick kittens they were when she brought them homes years before. She whispered to Stella how she must promise to not be so bossy with the other cats and to stop slapping the boys. And to all of them she spoke in hushed tones, too quiet for us to hear, private messages they only shared together.

Saturday Alisa quietly slipped into an unresponsive state. The oxygen machine would fill the room with a dull drone as the hospice nurses continually administered pain medicine and went about the efforts of keeping her comfortable.

In the early afternoon, suddenly and as if on cue, the cats who had kept vigil with Alisa all quietly left her side moving to unseen positions in the house. Her human family remained, including daughters Kari and Kalli, brother Charlie, her mother Dorothy, our church Pastor Bill LaMora and his wife Carol, along with assorted hospice nurses who were supporting us. Shortly after, surrounded by her human family, Alisa who had paced the floor so many times with a sick kitten in her arms, who had saved the lives of hundreds, loved and cared for so many orphaned cats and kittens, quietly took her last breath and left her earthbound life.

Somewhere in that moment in time, a beautiful garden gained a new angel. Alisa, who loved, tended and cared for so many helpless animals, life didn't end that Sunday afternoon. It had only just begun.

Later that week at Alisa's funeral service, daughter Kalli read the following prayer to the church which was filled to the brim. Alisa's contributions beyond rescue were evidenced by the rescue community in attendance in addition to people from Girl Scouts, church friends, co-workers and the many medical professionals who had treated and cared for her. Some of the most endearing people there were cancer survivors, many elderly veterans she had treated as a nurse, and patients' families. Kalli read above the tearful sounds of those present.

Do not stand at my grave and weep
I am not there; I do not sleep.
I am a thousand winds that blow,
I am the diamond glints on snow,
I am the sun on ripened grain,
I am the gentle autumn rain.
When you awaken in the morning's hush
I am the swift uplifting rush
Of quiet birds in circled flight.

I am the soft stars that shine at night.
Do not stand at my grave and cry,
I am not there; I did not die.

On the night of Alisa's death she came to me in a dream or perhaps a vision. She was walking upon the white sand of a beach wearing a long, snow blue and cream gown. She looked young and healthy, like she did in old photographs. Her favorite dog Tommy who had preceded her in death pranced happily along beside her, a piece of drift wood clamped in his mouth.

Looking towards me she said with a soft smile, "Everything is ok now," and saying those words she and Tommy joyfully walked down the beach and out of sight. The sense of calm and peace that came upon me showed that she was right.

Someday my journey in this life will also end. When given the choice I will proudly don my own robes in shades of blue, collect my kittens from the Blue Angel and in perfect peace, I will become the caretaker of my own Garden of Pets.

"The cat has always been associated with the moon. Like the moon it comes to life at night, escaping from humanity and wandering over housetops with its eyes beaming out through the darkness."

- Patricia Dale-Green

Epilogue

I began writing the story of the Blue Angel nearly five years ago following a special visit from an angelic spirit. I named her based on the colors in her robe. As I came to learn her earthbound name as Sarah, I also found the Blue Angel became a comforting messenger to me over the years. Through her teachings I have had the opportunity to share with others the message that the pets we have loved on earth await us on the other side.

The writing of *In Heaven Kittens Play* has been an emotional roller coaster for me over the years. Some parts of the book brought me pleasant thoughts and a smile, while others brought me sadness and heartache. But writing this book has taught me that the good far outweighs the bad.

Many fond memories have crossed my mind while I have sat late into the night writing. I can recall so many adoption events where orphaned, lonely cats and kittens found that one, true "forever home" waiting just for them. Excited children vying with one another for a position to hold the new addition to their family. Couples looking at the cats on display as one of them whispers how a third, purring member of the family is a good idea. And the image of both men and women, silently, often sobbing quietly as they warmly held a cat in their arms, knowing in their heart that a pet long past has chosen this day to return to them in a new body.

Bad memories also exist: A litter of kittens lost to disease; a beautiful cat taken by malnourishment or illness. Having to sit in the tomb-like silence of the veterinarian's office with a beloved cat you know you've taken there for the last time. An injection quietly ends its life and suffering and you return home having shed a river of tears with an empty pet carrier in the seat beside you.

But as the Blue Angel has taught me, when we mourn the death of a pet we tend to concentrate on the negative and not the blessing our pet has just received. In the twinkling of an eye the pain, discomfort and suffering of our furry loved one is gone. At that same moment in a garden too beautiful to describe, an angel waits patiently for their new arrival to join them. From that moment on, the pet we let cross over, lives an existence void of fear, hunger, abandonment and suffering. There with them for all eternity a devoted angel exists to provide them love, hugs and of course, a lap to sit on and two arms to hold them.

Look not on the death of a beloved pet as the

end but simply a transformation into something wonderful. A day will come when you will also make that journey to the other side and there your pets will be happily awaiting your return to them.

The above painting was executed by artist Dave Marak.
A full color rendition of this painting may be viewed at:

www.ccbpublishing.com/blueangel.html

About the Author

Nick Sacco started writing as a journalist for his high school paper in the small town of Cuba, Missouri. After graduation and a stint in the United States Marine Corps he continued as a contributing writer for newspaper and magazines plus worked as a radio disc jockey. Nick's writing would eventually go on an extended sabbatical while he worked as a police motorcycle officer in Kansas City, Missouri, retiring in 2004. Through his wife Alisa's work with Kansas City Siamese Rescue, Nick came into contact with hundreds of rescued cats and kittens. While no longer an animal rescue volunteer, Nick shares his home with a handful of beautiful cats and one overweight Cocker Spaniel, Buddy, who thinks he is a cat.

Visit Nick's web site:

www.nicksacco.com